A Life Lived

Elizabeth Hebert

Presentation by *BookLeaf Publishing*

Web: www.bookleafpub.com

E-mail: info@bookleafpub.com

ISBN: 9789357212052

First edition 2023

DEDICATION

I want to dedicate this book to my baby brother. Justin Andrew Fields. A life taken way to soon by the callousness of a coward.

To my mom,Robin,for always believing in me and encouraging me to do and be better.

To my niece, Rylee, for being an incredible young woman. I can only hope for the best life for you.

ACKNOWLEDGEMENT

I want to acknowledge the one that refused to save me but made me learn the best ways to save myself. The one that taught me that strength is found within, that we rule our own life,that we make our own happiness, and must do the things that make us our true self. Thank you Pine Trees.

PREFACE

This is a collections of poems that I have written about some of the moments in my life that have forced me to become stronger, happier, and more solid of a person. Some are about people that impacted my life and others about the feelings I have have expierenced. But all very realistic and true moments.

A Brother Lost

An early morning call
A break in the universe
An excessive cry
A forgotten flight to music city
A week of hurt, of pain, of tears
An emotional family
A lost flight back to home
A shuffle of rides
A night alone
A drive to clear my head
A week of numbness
A flight back to music city
A drive to get you
A song that broke me
A pack of your things
A drive back to mom's
A fight that broke what was left
A crack in a family
A lot more questions
A river of tears
A family left broken
A brother lost

Come to End

That dark counrty road should have been
peaceful.
The sun should have risen while you slept in
your bed.
Fishing poles should be loaded up and the boat
ready to go.
Potatoe salad and BBQ should be in the making.
The sweet tea chilling in the refrigerator.
The smoke and whiskey should be strong but
good.
The music loud and truthful.
The work day should be busy.
The time should be ticking away.
The fish should be bitting and the boat stay
floating.
The phone calls and the pictures should still be
made.
The truck should still be going.
The sun sitting as your coming home.
There never should have been a phone call
saying these things have come to an end.

The Moon

Many times it is just you and I.
Sitting here in the dark with only your light
shining.
My darkness is taking over so I sit with you to
absorb your light.
You shine the brightest when the darnkess
surrounds you.
Teaching me lessons of hope and strength.
You show me that no matter haw dark things do
get,
there is always a glow to help me through.
Your face shines on me and reminds me that it is
okay to dim.
You are the beacon of light that guides me
through my darkness.
When I feel lost and dark you pull me back to a
peaceful fight.

Words

words are not just words
words are not just said without thought
words put together can form a sentance
words together can bring a memory
words together can make you hate
words alone can make you cry
words can make you love
words can break your heart
words can teach a lesson
words will break the tension
words can bring you joy
words can end friendships
words can be twisted
words tell a story
words are more

The Beach

Bare feet running across the sand
Salty air being inhaled
Seagulls flying above
Fish flopping nearby
Sunny days and peaceful nights
Camp fires and roasted marshmallows
Waves crashing on the beach
I find my peace looking out across the sea
The never ending blue as the sea meets the sky
The fluffy clouds billowing by
The darkness of the night as the moon appears
It is the place I feel the comfort
The place I feel your spirit
The water grabbing me and drawing me in
The sand under my feet
The feel, the rush, the connection
The place that bring you back to this life

You

The little hairs of your mustache tickle with a
kiss
The way you wrap your arms around and just
pull me in
The look in your eyes as they pierce through my
heart
The way our fingers interlock and how I never
want to let go
The smell of you when my head rest on your
shoulder
The crook in your lip when you smile down at
me
The warmth of your embrace the encaspulates
my soul
The way you say my name or even when you
say nothing
The way we just fit together and the comfort we
find
The way you hand caresses as my fingers get
lost in your beard.
The taste of you that never seems to fade
The depths of your voice that just soothes me
The teeth that bite and send my senses crazy
The sound in your throat that drives me crazy
The passion that never fades.

A forgotten life

A father gone and a mother lost
A sister bitter and a brother younger
With heartace and confusion that never leaves.
The darkness that sits in the soul
the lost girl somewhere in the middle.

Broken promises and lies that burned
little faith could grow there.
Dark and empty rooms that could pierced the
light
Hidden in the cornor no hope left.

Hateful people and the lost girl
breaking her more than she can take.
For love and hope
She became used and abused.

Refusing to shine refusing to grow
She hid from the life that she knew.
Broken and hated, abused and betrayed
Darkness stronger than anyone could know.

Knives and blades wires and flames
She search for the pain to know she was.
Self inflected wounds would heal

Unwilling wounds never will.

Pain and lost in a world of hate
Darkness got stronger and hope diminished.
Life on the streets turned to a lesson
A drive to beat a darkness within.

The failed inflection of self distruction
Growing despise for a emotionless life.
Hatred and grief become a normal
Why look for light, or hope?

Running away and trying to change
Tent living to go back to nature.
A new start and a way to grow
Buring my past and letting go.

Fighting and striving to be
Lighting a candle and letting it blaze.
Finding a fire that set me free
Runnning from the dispair that once was me.

You Choose

You choose to pick it up,
But you blame others.
You choose to smoke that cigarette,
But you blame emotions.
You choose that drink,
But you blame your past.
You choose to hate,
But you blame me.
You choose to run,
But you blame her.
You choose to yell,
But you say I started it.
You choose to break it,
But you won't fix it.
You choose to be emotionless,
But you want compassion.
You choose others,
But want me to choose you.
You choose to be a hermit,
But you won't escape.
You choose to stop,
But get mad that I won't.
You choose hurt,
But I choose love.
You choose to leave,
But I fought to stay.

Dreams to Manifest

I never want to wake up from the dreams
You and I and ours together
Music and art all around
Two broken lives merged into one completely
Smiles and laughter
Love and hope
Dreams to manifest
Song of truth pour out as art colors the walls
Road trips and lazy days at home
Home cooked meal and dive bar diners
Saloons and bars and even sold out shows
Dreams to manifest
Chili and tortillas beer and smoke
Dogs playing in the yard
Music drifting out the windows
Warm embraces
Dreams to manifest
Happy days and amazing nights
Joyous morning and fruitful evenings
Loving life and growing old
Dreams to manifest

Escape was the only way

That little town beat me up
It broke my spirit and left me for broke
It killed my spirit and coked my voice.
My ears were deaf and my heart shattered.
Escape was the only way.
That boy was vicious.
He hit me and fought me.
Yelled and screamed in my face
Escape was the only way.
The house was gone and the food scarce.
The water was dirty and the baths were cold.
Broken and alone
Escape was the only way.
Guns and knives
Words of hate
Threats of death
Escape was the only way.

Home

The wooden panel walls were covered in photos
from years past.
The bookcases filled with trinkets stretched to
the ceiling.
The beige carpet caving under the pressure of
the old oak table.
The centerpiece with those tall candles never got
lit.
The kitchen smelled of Chicken and biscuits
The oven soon to hold that apple pie.
The old green couch covered with pillows.
The chairs full of people.
Doors opening as the kids run in and out.
Grandma yelling to keep the bugs out.
The old red picnic table doubled as a jungle
gym.
The garden full of tomatoes and peppers.
The old fence was long gone but the tree line
still stood.
The old grape vine on that small brown dirt
patch.
The garage packed with a crafter's dream.
The roses at the end of the drive.
The wooden swings on the back porch.
The old pie tin full of seed.
What I would do just to go home again.

Broken

Breaking into pieces it seems like no one cares.
Another day of a repeated cycle.
Breaking more with each passing moment
Moving on just seems so impossible.
Hope and trust have faded away.
Breaking with each passing second.
Emotionless overload has become reality.
Care and passion faded away.
A hopeful heart broken by you.
A dream shattered by your broken promises.
Not a day goes by that I do not feel broken.
Shattered, screaming, and crying I can't break
free.
I don't want to break
I want to live and thrive
But you keep breaking me down on this repeated
cycle of hell
The dreams will return and the hope will
flourish
One day I will prove you tried but you didn't
leave me broken.

Music

The music reaches out and grabs my soul
It smooths out the wrinkles of hate and anguish
Making the pressures slowly fade to normal
My heart matches the beat.

The smooth voice singing those words,
Calm my thoughts and easy my nerves.
Bringing my me back to reality
My head matches the beat

The constant beat of the drums,
Bring a safe thump of consciousness.
Taking me back to the solitude of the moment
My breath matches the beat.

The strumming on that guitar,
Brings the refreshing clarity
Giving my head time to renew
My brain slowly matches the beat.

The music encompasses completely
Giving me my life back.
I match the beat.

Paint

Vivid colors of that creamy paste
Spread over the stark white.
Meshing and mixing and become something
more.
A vision of colors joining together
Creating a mystery for the senses to entangle
The nerves enlighten and the hues mixing
The blues and greens, reds and yellows
Combining the vision with the thought
Creating a masterpieces if just for myself
Letting it out creating my crazy
The purples and pinks, black and greys
Mingled together and exposing my mind
The white becomes vivid
The calm become chaotic
My thoughts on a canvas
My mind empty.

Leaving

See the look of the man,
I think he's angry.

He finds it hard to see the ace,
Overshadowed by the compassionate face.

Who is that standing near his guitar?
I think she'd like to hear him sing.

She is but a thundery traveler,
Admired as she gazes upon the moon.

Her passionate cry is just a coyote,
It needs no emotion, it runs on commotion.

She's not alone she brings a dog,
a book, and lots of laughter.

She likes to talk to the raven,
Especially one that's in the garden.

The man shudders at the interesting beer
He want to leave but the fear.

Leaving her there.

I Sit

The darkness that hits around 2am
with the small sparkles lighting up the sky
I sit there in thought.

The freedom of not seeing what is there
the blank canvas that just grows
I sit there in thought.

The fresh night air takes the sadness
it turns it to the happiest calm
I sit there in thought.

The clouds slowly passing through the sky
the changes in hues settle my thoughts
I sit there in thought.

Whiskey

Whose whiskey is that? I think I know.
Its owner is quite sad though.
It really is a tale of woe,
I watch him frown. I cry hello.
He gives his whiskey a shake,
And sobs until the tears make.
The only other sound's the break,
Of distant waves and birds awake.
The whiskey is intense, sarcastic and deep,
But he has promises to keep,
Until then he shall not sleep.
He lies in bed with ducts that weep.
He rises from his bitter bed,
With thoughts of sadness in his head,
He idolises being dead.
Facing the day with never ending dread.

I look

With the world crumbling down around me
I look to the moon to find a friend
When the skies darken
I look to the stars to find some light
With the crashing of the waves beating me down
I look to the sand for a place to anchor
When the winds blow me down
I look to the dirt to ground me
When my dreams are crushed
I look to the seed to grow me
When the voice is silenced
I look for the song of the raven
When the emotions eat at me
I look for the cry of the coyote
When lost in the mind
I look for the clarity in the stream

www.ingramcontent.com/pod-product-compliance
Lightning Source LLC
LaVergne TN
LVHW041300200726
843507LV00014B/3064

Brilliance

She does not know any better
She believes she is more creative than me

They do not know any better

I am a brilliant, creative, being.

Novel

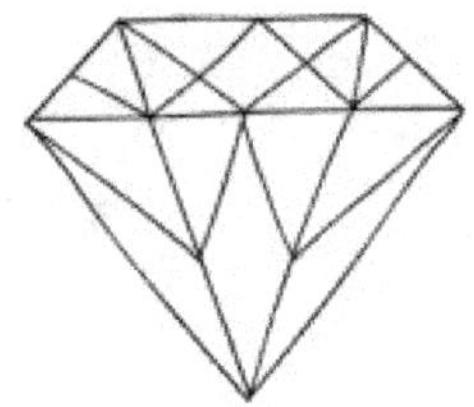

Black women we are novel
Outstanding and unique

One day they will notice
But they will be too late

We are One
of a kind

Our beauty is ours
Our treasure divine

Petit Paquet

My Whole Word
in a
little package

My
True Love

Dancing Feet

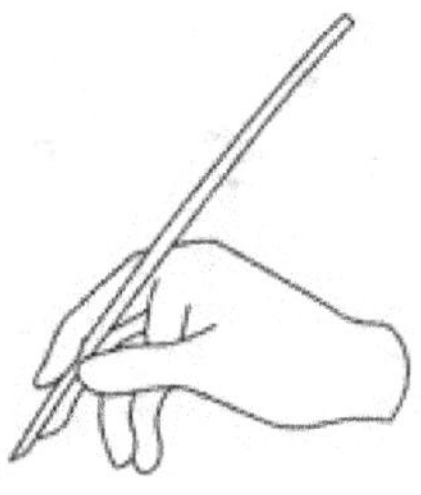

I have danced
on floors
much too hot
for feet

Its a shade
A layer
of Me

My Mind

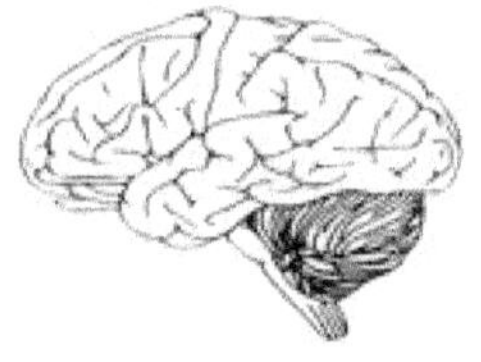

My mind________
Is a maze.
Very organized.
Hard to get through.

There's no guide.
No map.

I have barely escaped myself

Resilience

My ability to be a wife, mother & sister all at
once
A woman still soft yet hard all at once

The warmth of the sun
The ice of the seas
The flexibility of water

As sweeping as the wind

Every day I wake up a woman.
Every day I still win.

Morning Prayer

I pray my children never feel like
I have so many problems

They can't come to me about their own

- A Mama

Our Hair

My hair defies gravity
It is stubborn shiny strong

You will not make me damage it

You will not make me ashamed

Our hair is unpredictable
Yet,
Beautiful, truly a force

It does not matter that it is different
That it is not the same as yours

Tis The Season

Tis the season to be joyful
Tis the season full of love
Tis the season of depression of deception and of
drugs

Tis the season for reflection
and acknowledging who you are
Tis the season for distant friendships and visiting
family near and far

It's the season of new year new me
A season of fresh possibilities

It's the season of "Will you marry me?"
and "my best friend really hasn't been there for
me"

It's the season to be forgiving and accepting
everyone for who they are

Tis the season for setting boundaries,
remembering your worth and setting the bar

Mythology

Like I'm trapped in the grasp of Charybdis
Like I've been struck by the lightening of Zeus
Like I've been hit with Cupid's arrow
My love for you is overwhelmingly true

Tick Tock

This is not about you
You are letting your brokenness show
Be supportive
Be a friend
Trust that your time will come

Memory Lane

I remember being under quarantine
I remember falling back in love

I remember being isolated
I remember grocery shopping with gloves

I remember being scared and nervous
I remember finally feeling free

I remember fully working remote
I remember having time for me

E

This is your season, Rebirth, Redemption, Anew
They will try to stop you
You can't
Be stopped
Embrace who you are becoming
This season
Will be
Beautiful
Welcome to your enlightening euphoric
evolution

I'm a Fan

I'm a fan of my friend whose a lawyer
My homegirl passed the bar the first time

I'm a fan of my friend with the business
A mother
of three
still a dime

I'm a fan of my future professor
She's a newlywed
Just bought a home

I'm a fan of my gemstone
She's special
With a heart truly made out of gold

Got a friend whose an actress
A Diva

I know someday she will be a star

I'm surrounded by excellent women
I'm inspired by all that they are

Spoken Word From a Feminist

Shine bright baby girl
But don't shine more than me

Be bold, be daring
But remember you're not free

You will work just as hard, maybe harder it is
true
But the reality is that there is nothing you can do

Now I don't say this to discourage you, I only
speak the truth

But the world is not changing, as far as I can see

These words were once spoken by a "feminist"
to me.

Barefoot in The Grass

You are Alive
Be grateful for the gift of life
Smile often, and laugh ridiculously
Run barefoot in the grass

Exceed your own expectations
The only one who can stop you is

you

Time is absolutely priceless
Make room for the real you

Sorry to All The Megs

Why is it that when we tell our story, it is so
hard for you all to believe?

Why do you all think it is okay to drag us?
The only human beings that can conceive.

You all have consistently played games
Well I have some news for you

I know my worth
I will fight back
I won't make it easy for you

Lady Boss

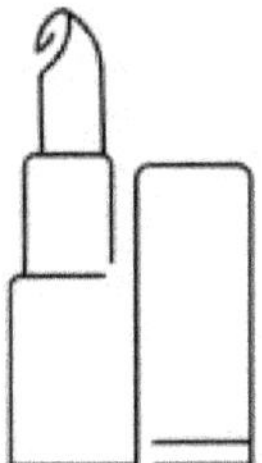

Lady Boss -
A living display of what happens when a woman uses their God-given gifts and does what they love in excellence.

www.ingramcontent.com/pod-product-compliance
Lightning Source LLC
La Vergne TN
LVHW041300200726

843507LV00014B/3065